A Useful
Spelling Handbook For Adults

I have had many years of experience in teaching adults and post-school learners in Adult Basic Education, Further Education and various other education settings. Almost universally, I have found that the main two problems affecting adults with poor literacy skills are learning how to use punctuation, and learning how to spell. This applies particularly to dyslexic adults, but also to a huge range of people in this age group who, for a wide variety of reasons, have trouble with spelling.

In this book, I have used the same approach as when I teach people face-to-face how to spell, and I hope that readers and users of "A Useful Spelling Handbook" will enjoy having the next thing to "personal tuition" as they work their way through the different spelling rules and patterns and emerge as better spellers.

Further advice and help for dyslexic adults can be found in a separate book, "A Useful Dyslexia Handbook for Adults".

A Useful
Spelling Handbook For Adults

Catherine Taylor

A Useful
Spelling Handbook For Adults

Olympia Publishers

www.olympiapublishers.com
OLYMPIA PAPERBACK EDITION

Copyright © Catherine Taylor 2009

A CIP catalogue record for this title is
available from the British Library.

ISBN: 978-1-84897-031-1

Olympia Publishers part of Ashwell Publishing Ltd

First Published in 2009

Olympia Publishers
60 Cannon Street
London
EC4N 6NP

Printed in Great Britain

Dedication

"To all my wonderful colleagues, past and present".

CONTENTS

Introduction

Why adults have trouble with spelling

For a long number of years I have been teaching basic literacy skills, including that of spelling, to learners in the post-16 and adult age range. In this time I have come across a great variety of reasons why adults – who have usually spent over ten years being educated in school – experience trouble with spelling. Sometimes there is one particular reason for this, which is easy to isolate. In other cases, different factors are involved. The end result, however, is the same. Spelling can be a nightmare for these people, and poor spelling can affect such things as job prospects, educational progression, self-esteem and daily life in general.

How "good spelling" is acquired

Readers of "A Useful Dyslexia Handbook for Adults" will recall the section about reading and spelling, where I explained that reading, and more especially spelling, are two of the most complex skills which the brain is required to carry out. Greatly simplified, we can consider that the following skills are needed for good spelling:

- The ability to remember the name of each individual letter and the sound(s) of each individual letter, e.g. **a**, **b**, **c**, where the sound of each of these letters is different to their name, and where '**a**' can have a short or a long sound.
- The ability to remember the sound(s) of combinations of letters, and where to use these, e.g. '**ear**' in **hear, heart, earth, pear**.

- The ability to remember the rules of spelling, e.g. if you add a 'silent e' to the word 'tap', it will change the sound of the '**a**' to that in 'tape'.
- The ability to remember the exceptions to the rules of spelling, for example '**ch**' sounds like the beginning and ending of the word 'church' – but in the word 'chemist' it sounds like a '**c**' or a '**k**', and in the word 'charade' it sounds like '**sh**'.
- The ability to remember which sounds translate into which shapes, and string these together rapidly to write onto paper or type onto a word-processor.
- The ability to remember the shape and appearance of whole words, or parts of whole words, so that these can be recognised on sight, and recalled from memory to be written onto paper or typed onto a word-processor.

You can see that a lot of memory is involved, as well as learning these complex encoding skills and the physical ability to represent them in writing.

Unsatisfactory or missing education
The place for learning these - amongst many other - skills is normally in school. There can be many reasons why adults missed out on their education in childhood and adolescence. For instance, their attendance pattern might have been poor or sporadic. Perhaps there were social, medical or behavioural problems which interfered with the learning process.

If a person's school education was missing, inadequate or unsatisfactory, there is the strong possibility that this has had an impact on their ability to spell.

Learning difficulties and dyslexia
Clearly, for individuals with a general learning difficulty, this will affect the learning of spelling along with the learning of everything else.

This is not the case for people with a Specific Learning Difficulty (dyslexia). These individuals may be very bright and able to learn things quickly, but they are likely to have difficulty with written language, in reading and even more so in spelling. More detailed information on these spelling problems, and help in overcoming them, can be found in "A Useful Dyslexia Handbook for Adults". It is worth noting that adults with a poor visual memory will have difficulty with remembering the shape and appearance of whole words and will tend to spell words as they sound; whilst adults with a poor auditory memory will have difficulty in relating letters to sounds, and will often try to "guess" at the spellings they need to use.

The English Language
The story of the development and growth of the English language is a long and fascinating one, much too detailed to be explained in a book of this size. However, a very simplified look at this will help you to understand why English spelling can be so difficult for you.

You can perhaps see that in more "phonetic" languages such as Russian or Italian, where there is one letter to represent one sound, encoding the different sounds into letters and then into words is much easier to deal with.

Language shifts and changes all the time, and English has had more than its fair share of historic influences and developments. On the plus side, these have greatly enriched our language so that, for example, we have an abundant choice of words available to describe many individual concepts and ideas. For instance, instead of saying you are 'tired', you could say that you are weary, exhausted, fatigued, shattered, drained, worn out and so on. You could be happy, overjoyed, elated, pleased, delighted, cheerful, and various other descriptions of your state of mood.

On the minus side, these diverse influences mean that we have different ways of representing sounds, so that, for example, the same sound can be written as '**there**', '**their**' or '**they're**'. Conversely, we have already seen that the same letters can give us different sounds, e.g. note the different sound of the '**ou**' in **cloud**, **group**, **borough**, **cough**, **tough**; and the '**gh**' in **borough**, **cough**, **slough**, **eight**, and **ghost**.

The early language of the British Isles survives in northern and western areas in the Celtic languages of Scots and Irish Gaelic, and the language of the Cymry Celts in Welsh and the remnants of Cornish. Little is left in England of these languages, but they can be traced in place names and descriptions, e.g. Thames, tor, Brockholes. The Romans came and went, but did not leave much language from their occupation period in Britain. Latin words were to appear much later in the language at several different time periods.

If we consider the different invasions and influxes of people coming into the British Isles, it is not difficult to see why there are so many different influences on the language, and on spelling. The Anglo-Saxons brought the basis of English and its grammar as we know it, followed by the Vikings whose language had similarities and was mutually intelligible. Some of their words were identical, and in other instances there were similar but recognisable words for things of the same meaning. For example in Old English, to describe a smock-type garment, there was the Anglo-Saxon word 'scyrte' ('sc' beng pronounced as 'sh') which evolved into the Modern English word 'shirt'; and Viking 'skyrta', which developed into the Modern English word 'skirt'.

The Norman Conquest, in its turn, introduced a heavy French input, while Greek and some Spanish words entered the language at a later period – each with their own ways of representing sounds.

In later times other immigrant populations have arrived, bringing yet more patterns of spelling which might seem not to match with English spelling conventions, for instance 'spaghetti', 'yoghurt', 'tikka', 'vodka'.

A variety of other factors has also influenced English spelling patterns, for example the invention of the printing press and the standardisation of English. Changes to the language and unusual spellings continue to arrive through developments in science, culture, technology and life in general…for instance, fifty years ago what on earth would we have made of an 'i-pod'?

Other reasons for difficulty with spelling

Less common reasons for difficulty with spelling, but which nevertheless should be mentioned, include such factors as the incidence of adults who have had a stroke or suffered a head injury at some point. For these people, learning – or re-learning – to spell may be difficult and prolonged, but in my experience it is by no means impossible.

This book

Whatever your reason for having trouble with spelling, I am confident that this book can help you.

We are fortunate in the present times to have technology which helps us with spelling in the form of pocket and computer spell-checkers. These are valuable tools indeed, and do have an important part to play for those with spelling problems, as well as enabling people to produce a tidy and legible script. Repeatedly seeing the correct spelling of a word is beneficial, and will undoubtedly help with the memorisation of spellings. However, if you have trouble with spelling, it can be difficult knowing which of the word options you need to select electronically. Technology alone is not the answer.

I hope you enjoy working through the exercises in 'A Useful Spelling Handbook For Adults', and that it will be a useful book to have on hand to help with **your** spelling.

Alphabetical order

Here is the alphabet in capital (upper case) letters:

A B C D E F G H I J K L M N O P Q R S T U V W X Y Z

Here is the alphabet in small (lower case) letters:

a b c d e f g h i j k l m n o p q r s t u v w x y z

Before you start to improve your spelling, it is important for you to know the alphabet, recognise the upper and lower case letters, and know what order the alphabet is in.

1.

a) Take a sheet of paper. Write out the alphabet in large **upper case** letters. Cut these out. Mix them up on a desk or table top. Re-arrange them in alphabetical order. Keep doing this until you feel confident that you know the order of the alphabet in **upper case** letters.

b) Take a sheet of paper. Write out the alphabet in large **lower case** letters. Cut these out. Mix them up on a desk or table top. Re-arrange them in alphabetical order. Keep doing this until you feel confident that you know the order of the alphabet in **lower case** letters.

c) Now arrange all the upper case letters in alphabetical order, and match the lower case letters to their capitals. Keep doing this until you feel confident that you recognise the upper and lower case alphabet.

2.   You will have noticed that in a dictionary or telephone directory, the words or names are listed in the order of the alphabet. Arrange these lists in alphabetical order:

a)   orange
cherry
banana
apple
strawberry
tangerine
pear
lemon

b)   cat
giraffe
elephant
mouse
dog
tiger
ostrich
rat
frog
horse

c)   Ben
Zoe
Callum
Leanne
Jane
Ann
Taz
Shaheen

d)   Jones
Smith
Lenski
McDonald

Cliffe
Anderson
Kauser
Davis
Everett
Wilson

Now let's make things a little more difficult.
Sometimes, in a list of words or names, you have more than one item beginning with the same letter. To put these into alphabetical order, you arrange them by the order of the second letter in the word. For example, look at the names of these cities:

Manchester	Newcastle
London	Dublin
Leeds	Cardiff
Bradford	Sheffield
Belfast	Birmingham

Re-arranged in alphabetical order, these are:

Belfast
Birmingham
Bradford
Cardiff
Dublin
Leeds
London
Manchester
Newcastle
Sheffield

3.   Re-arrange these lists into alphabetical order:

a)   England
        Austria
        Germany

Ireland
France
America
Finland
Iceland

b)   DIY
Football boots
Sportswear
Dinner sets
Fridges
Shower curtains
Dining tables
Shoes
Fragrances
Schoolwear

4.   If the first two letters of different words in a list are the same, you arrange them in order of the third letter. If the first three letters of different words in a list are the same, you arrange them in order of the fourth letter.
Re-arrange these lists into alphabetical order:

c)   cordial
milk
cola
tea
coffee
water
cocoa
Cappuccino

d)   Hull
Chesterfield
Thetford
Huntingdon
Bridgwater
Thirsk

Bradford
Bridgend
Chester
Huddersfield

Take care when arranging names beginning with 'Mac' or 'Mc'.

In the BT telephone directory, 'Mac' and 'Mc' are treated as exactly the same, represented in upper case letters, and the names are listed in the order of the letter which comes after the 'C', e.g. MACCABE, MCDONALD, MACKINTOSH. In some indexing systems, however, such as dictionaries, Mc and Mac are treated as 'Mac', and otherwise these names appear in order of the letters, e.g. Mackintosh, MacLean, MacLeod, McLuhan, MacMahon.

With names beginning with O + apostrophe, the apostrophe is usually ignored for indexing purposes. E.g. Oates, O'Brien, Ollerenshaw, O'Shea.

Where there are two or more of the same surnames listed, use the initial of the first name (if this is shown) in alphabetical order.

5.   List these names in alphabetical order. You might find it helpful to first group together any names beginning with the same letter. Treat 'Mac' and 'Mc' as 'Mac', and list them by the letter after the 'c'.

Moss, J
Sutton, M
Jackson, P
Jacks, S
McDonald, A
Sutton, D
Jackson, O

Burley, W
Walshaw, C
Ali, M
MacDonald, J
Alderson, G
Walton, R
Johnson, P
Jones, K
Oates, M
O'Neill, M
Mackie, F
Oakes, S
Anderson, A
Chan, P
Mackintosh, G

a or an?

First of all you need to know about <u>vowels</u>.

The five vowels in the alphabet are:

a   e   i   o   u

Each of these letters is a sound made with the mouth open. All the other letters are sounds made with using the lips and tongue and teeth.

y is not a vowel, but sometimes it *seems* like a vowel, in words such as cry, berry.

All the other letters are called <u>consonants</u>.
(a) **b c d** (e) **f g h** (i) **j k l m n** (o) **p q r s t** (u) **v w x y z**

If a word begins with a <u>vowel</u>, you use **'an'**.

e.g. an **e**gg, an **o**wl, an **a**pple.

If a word begins with a <u>consonant</u>, you use **'a'**.

e.g. a **c**at, a **t**able, a **z**ip.

However, you need to take care with words beginning with 'h'.

If the '**h**' is sounded, use '**a**': a horse, a hat, a horror story.
If the '**h**' is silent, use '**an**': an hour, an honour.

Also, take care with the word '**one**'. In this word the first vowel (**o**) sounds like a consonant (w). Use '**a**' with this: **a** one-hour film.

1. Write 'a' or 'an' in the gaps:

a) ___ letter
b) ___ owl
c) ___ chair
d) ___ pen
e) ___ orange
f) ___ banana
g) ___ horse
h) ___ map
i) ___ honest man
j) ___ hour or two
k) ___ half-hour
l) ___ hopeful letter

2. In the following piece, put 'a' or 'an' in the gaps:

Last week I went to ___ different supermarket for ___ change. I found ___ empty parking space straight away. Then I got ___ trolley. I was pleased to find that there was ___ small one, which is better for ___ person like me who doesn't need ___ lot of things.
I got ___ lettuce, ___ cucumber and ___ onion to make ___ salad. Then I filled ___ bag with carrots. I decided I wanted ___ apple, so I got ___ few.
I went to get ___ loaf of bread and saw that I could get ___ hot pie. I also got ___ bottle of milk and ___ packet of butter, which was ___ low-fat type. I was pleased to see ___ lot of meals with ___ one-person sized helping.

Then I noticed it was raining, so I bought ___ umbrella. On the way out I saw I could get ___ magazine and ___ newspaper. I had ___ look at my watch, and saw I'd been ___ hour in there. That was ___ real surprise!

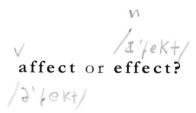

affect or effect?

These two words are very easy to confuse, although the sound of them is different.

'effect' is a noun (naming word) and its meaning is 'the result of something'.
Examples:
The illness had a bad **effect** on him.
The dim light created a strange **effect**.

'affect' is a verb (doing word) and its meaning is when something has an *effect* on something else.
Examples:
The bad weather might **affect** attendance.
Watching too much TV might **affect** your eyesight.

1. In the following sentences, fill in the gaps with **effect** or **affect**.

a) Taking too much time off work could _____ your job.
b) Watching a sad film always has a bad _____ on me.
c) Sad films _____ me too.
d) This medication has one very strong side _____.
e) The holiday has had a remarkable _____ on her.
f) Too much sun can _____ your skin.
g) Sun and rain together create a beautiful _____ called a rainbow.
h) Bright lights do _____ me.
i) I do not allow bad weather to _____ me.

j) The theatre company used green lighting to create an eerie _____.

2. Complete the following, using the word **affect, affects, affected** or **effect** to fill the gaps.

I had a big meal late last night which _____ me badly. The _____ of it was terrible. I could not sleep, and when I did drop off, I had vivid dreams with a cinema-type _____. I told my friend how I had been _____. She told me that too much food late at night always _____ her, too.

al, el or le?

These word-endings are very similar and it is often difficult to know which one to use. There is no spelling rule. Instead you have to remember these as you come to them.

The *sound* of these endings is slightly different. Try sounding-out these words, and take careful notice of the difference in sound:

sandal   **shovel**   **candle**

Fill in the missing words in these sentences, choosing between -al, -el, or –le.

a) I'm going to see my auntie and u_____ next week.
b) Shake the liquid, and then wait for it to s_____ down.
c) You might not agree with each other, but please try not to qu _____.
d) A c_____ is a creature with one or two humps which lives in the desert.
e) The coloured part of a flower is called the p_____.
f) My sister collects m_____ cars.
g) My dog is very soft and g_____.
h) I've got toothache so I will make a d_____ appointment.
i) Shall I fill the k_____ and we can have a hot drink?
j) Close the door please, using the h_____.
k) A th_____ is a very prickly plant.
l) Many clocks have a d_____ display.

Apostrophe s, verb s or plural s?
(Also other uses of the apostrophe)

When you are making a singular noun (naming word) into a plural by adding an 's', there is <u>never</u> an apostrophe. For example:

I have a dog and two **cats**.
I have one sister and two **brothers**.
There are three **assignments** to do.

1. Make each of the singular words underlined into a plural by adding an 's':

a)   I will buy the <u>meal.</u>
b)   She is going to look at the <u>room</u>.
c)   I eat <u>cereal</u> every day.
d)   Which <u>carpet</u> do you like best?
e)   Which <u>job</u> are you interested in?
f)   I've hurt my <u>leg</u>.
g)   Remember to pull out the <u>plug</u>.
h)   Don't forget to pick up the <u>key</u>.
i)   They sat in the shade of the <u>tree</u>.
j)   Can you switch on the <u>light</u>, please?

When you are using a verb (doing word) that ends in an 's', there is <u>never</u> an apostrophe. For example:

Our shop **sells** everything.
This tutor **gives** a good lesson.
The canteen **provides** a decent meal.

2. Find a verb (one word only) which ends in 's' to fit the gaps in each of these sentences. Remember, there is no apostrophe.

a)   That car _____ a good wash.
b)   Jack _____ a different language.
c)   The shop _____ at half past nine.
d)   Ashley _____ his dog for a walk every day.
e)   Arshad _____ a chocolate bar every morning.
f)   Karen _____ a lot of coffee.
g)   He always _____ us laugh.
h)   She _____ the car slowly.
i)   The telephone _____ all the time.
j)   Oliver always _____ a big breakfast.

The 'apostrophe s' is used to show 'possession' of, or 'belonging to', something. For example:

My mate's flat is near here = **The flat belonging to my mate** is near here.
My dad's car is old = **The car belonging to my dad** is old.
Her mother's name is Nina = **The name belonging to her mother** is Nina.

3. Only one of the words in bold print in each sentence needs an apostrophe. Which is it? Put in the apostrophe.

a)   They searched the **lists** to find the **mans** name.
b)   We took **boots, coats, hats** and thick **socks** for our **weeks** holiday.
c)   Kevin always **sulks** when he **sees** his **brothers** car.
d)   Our **cat** sleeps in the **dogs** basket.
e)   There is **always** the **tutors** book which **tells** us the **answers**.
f)   He **says** he **knows** the **childrens names**.
g)   **Jessicas** mum **likes carrots, peas** and **cabbage**.

32

Sulk atn empolul ?

h)　　He never **reads yesterdays newspapers.**
i)　　Tim **plays** the piano but never touches his **sisters** guitar.
j)　　The phone **rings** all the time in **Toms** office.

Beware! There is another use of the apostrophe! This is to show that a letter, or letters, are missing. It can be confusing, especially where there are other shortened parts of the word. For example:

I **can't** go = I **can not** go.
There **won't** be any food left for us = There **will not** be any food left for us.
The **show's** over = The **show is** over.
That **dog's** nasty = That **dog is** nasty.
Sam's gone to the football match = **Sam has** gone to the football match.

4. Write out these sentences with the apostrophe words in full:

a)　　You'll never learn.
b)　　I know he'll win.
c)　　There's only a day left.
d)　　I can't come.
e)　　That's life.
f)　　He won't do as he's told.
g)　　I'll ring you.
h)　　I didn't know that.
i)　　He doesn't know either.
j)　　I wouldn't go into town if I were you.
k)　　She couldn't climb the stairs.
l)　　I shan't ring her.
m)　　What's the title of that book?
n)　　There'll never be another like it.

as or has?

The sound of these two words is different, but some accents pronounce them nearly the same.

To work out which of these words you need, try using the word 'had'. If it makes sense, you need 'has' in your sentence. Otherwise, choose 'as'.

For example:
He ? a red sports car.
He **had** a red sports car. (This makes sense.)
He **has** a red sports car.

She ? a long way to go.
She **had** a long way to go. (This makes sense.)
She **has** a long way to go.

He is ? tall ? his brother.
He is **had** tall **had** his brother. (This does not make sense.)
He is **as** tall **as** his brother.

1. Fill in the missing words in these sentences, choosing 'as' or 'has'.

a)   He ___ been to the cinema with me.
b)   The film was very good, ___ we expected.
c)   My brother Jack ___ a very good MP3 player.
d)   He ___ lived there for a very long time.
e)   I saw the castle ___ we drove past.
f)   There ___ never been a better time.

g)   Laura ___ a very good job.
h)   He was there ___ quick ___ a flash.
i)   He ___ given me a lovely present.
j)   Could I have some more cake, please, ___ it's my birthday?

2. Complete the following, using **as** or **has**.

___ there ___ been very little interest in the soup, it ___ been decided to take this off the canteen menu. It ___ also been noted that there are not ___ many people buying salad ___ last year, so the manager ___ made the decision to serve this ___ a side dish. Nothing else ___ been changed.

[handwritten notes:]

as : como... ,

tan, tanto(s) tanta(s) ... como as ... as salv.

como ...

ya que j)

Cu ándo? e) conj ¹⁾ while something else is
mientras ?   =   happening
         I saw the castle as we drove past
c/ in the way in which . the film was very good, as we
as : prep, salv, conj   expected .

35

b or d?

People with a specific spelling difficulty may have trouble with **b** and **d**. If this is one of your problems, try this section.

Here is a 'tip' to help you see if you have b and d the right way round.

Write down the word **bed** – if you've got it right, it will look like the shape of a bed. If not, it doesn't look like anything special.

bed ✔   **deb** x   **ded** x

The sound of '**b**' is made with your lips pressed together. The sound of '**d**' is made with your tongue touching the roof of mouth at the front.

1. Are these words correct? What should they be?

	Word	Correct? YES or NO	Should be:
a)	duddles		
b)	dabble		
c)	Brabford		
d)	robbed		
e)	bramdles		
f)	candle		
g)	fadulous		
h)	Dudlin		
i)	soba water		

k)	cupdoard		
l)	stadle		
m)	cubble		

2. Put the missing letter (**b** or **d**) into these words:

a)   groun_
b)   _efore
c)   _e_t
d)   can_le
e)   _a_y
f)   rose_u_
g)   stoppe_
h)   ta_let
i)   _a_ger
j)   _e_room

Compound Words

There are some words in English which *look* long and difficult, but when we study them, we find that they are actually made up of two or more words put together.

Once we split these long words up into two parts, they are much easier to cope with.

Examples
Strawberry = straw + berry
sunshine = sun + shine
landlord = land + lord
breakfast = break + fast
headlight = head + light   Get the idea?

1. Split these compound words into two single words.

a)   lighthouse
b)   railway
c)   butterfly
d)   waterproof
e)   tablecloth
f)   windscreen   *parebrisis*
g)   nobody
h)   Iceland
i)   newspaper
j)   friendship
k)   motorway
l)   pineapple
m)   blackmail   *chantye, extorsion*

38

n) breakfast
o) earwig — _oscanchn_ n. Tijereta insect
p) carpet
q) buttercup
r) tappet — n. mecánica vástigo, tapué
s) toothache
t) forklift — n. Tro, carretilla elevadora, montacargas

2. Match the words in the first list with the words in the second list.
Write out your new words.

New words

a) wind   quarters
b) country   line
c) black   net
d) data   times
e) head   board
f) out   screen
g) inter   base
h) clock   side
i) cup   bird
j) horse   wise
k) bath   shoe
l) over   graph
m) photo   room
n) some   take

3. Now try these:

New words

a) under   sheet
b) eye   paste
c) tooth   load
d) no   proof
e) some   berry
f) hope   where
g) spread   less
h) goose   ball
i) fool   look

39

j) butter   stand
k) grand   fly
l) friend   thing
m) over   ship
n) out   father

4. Sometimes the same thing happens in place names. Try these:

<u>Place names</u>

a) Black   ham
b) Corn   pool
c) Wake   shire
d) New   wall
e) Old   field
f) York   castle

5. Can you find a word to add to these, to make a new compound word? Write out your new words.

a) life   g) hedge   m) rail
b) grand   h) table   n) cup
c) grape   i) back   o) night
d) straw   j) head   p) wood
e) pea   k) sea   q) moon
f) sun   l) fire   r) stair

hedgehog erizo

Consonants

Consonants are all the letters in the alphabet which are **not** vowels.

These are:
b c d f g h j k l m n p q r s t v w x y z

The sound of each of these letters is made with your lips, tongue and teeth.

The <u>vowels</u> are: **a e i o u**

Which vowels could you put into these spaces between these consonants, to make them into words?

a)   w_nd_w
b)   t_ _th
c)   t_l_v_s_ _n
d)   p_nc_l
e)   b_ttl_
f)   b_sk_t
g)   l_ght
h)   d_nn_r
i)   k_tt_n
i)   b_thr_ _m
j)   b_n_n_
k)   t_bl_t
l)   l_dyb_rd
m)   s_g_r
n)   m_s_c
o)   w_g_n

p)   s_p_rm_rk_t
q)   m_tch_s
r)   p_ _c_ck
s)   f_ _tb_ll

Double trouble

First of all: Do you know what a **suffix** is? It is a bit joined on to the end of a word, such as −**ed**, −**ing**, −**ful**.
When adding a suffix, it is confusing trying to decide whether or not to double the last letter of a word.

SHORT WORDS

If you are adding a <u>consonant suffix</u> (a suffix beginning with a consonant) to a word, never double the last letter.
hope, **hopeful**
late, **lately**
neat, **neatly**
thank, **thankful**

If you are adding a <u>vowel suffix</u> (a suffix beginning with a vowel) to a word, there are general rules you can follow:

<u>Words with a short vowel sound ending in one consonant</u>
If the vowel sound is 'short' or 'hard' and the word ends in one consonant (as in cat, beg, pot, ban, stop) the last letter should be doubled when adding a <u>vowel suffix</u>.
<u>Examples</u>
stop, **stopped, stopping, stopper**
pat**, patted, patting**
beg, **begged, begging, beggar**
grit, **gritted, gritting, gritter**

Note: This rule does not apply to words ending in 'x'.

Words with a short vowel sound ending in two consonants

If the vowel sound is "short" and the word ends in two consonants (as in past, cost, raft), do not double the last letter when adding a vowel suffix.

Examples

cost, **costing, costed**

camp, **camped, camping, camper**

Words with a long vowel sound

If the vowel sound is "long" or "soft", e.g. as in seal, fate, cloud, do not double the final letter when adding a vowel suffix **(If there is a silent e, you need to remove this first).**

Examples

sail, **sailed, sailing, sailor**

howl, **howled, howling, howler**

cool, **cooled, cooling, cooler**

hope, **hoped, hoping**

LONGER WORDS

Where there is more than one syllable, you need to check where the stress falls in the word. For example:

Under**stand** – stress falls on the last syllable

For**give** – stress falls on the last syllable

Laminate – stress falls on the first syllable

Gallop – stress falls on the first syllable

Decorate – stress falls on the first syllable

Be**gin** – stress falls on the last syllable

Re**fer** – stress falls on the last syllable

La**ment** – stress fall on the last syllable

Com**mit** – stress falls on the last syllable

Benefit – stress falls on the first syllable

Em**barr**ass – stress falls on the second syllable

Arr**ange** – stress falls on the last syllable

Com**pel** – stress falls on the last syllable

Got the idea?

If the stress does not fall on the last syllable, never double the last letter of the word, whatever type of suffix you are adding.

If the stress falls on the last syllable, you can use the general rules set out above for short words, applying them to the final syllable. There are a few words where the final syllable sounds 'long' but ends in one vowel + one consonant, e.g. 'control'. We treat these as if the sound of the last syllable was short – i.e. control, controller, controlling, controlled.

If a word ends in 'e', remember to remove this before adding a <u>vowel suffix</u>.

Understand, **understanding, understandable**
Forgive, **forgiver, forgiving**
Begin, **beginner, beginning**
Refer, **referral, referring, referred**
Lament, **lamenting, lamented**
Commit, **committed, committing, commitment**
Arrange, **arranged, arranging**
Compel, **compelling, compelled**

1. Add as many <u>consonant suffixes</u> (e,g, -less, -ness, –ful, -ly) as you can to each of these words. Do not double the last letter.

a) hope   b) dim
c) glad   d) fat
e) kind   f) bad
g) short   h) joy
i) mad   j) tact

2. Add as many <u>vowel suffixes</u> (e.g. –ing, –er, –ed, –able) as you can to each of these words. Double the last letter **only** where the vowel sound is short.

a) pat	b) bet
c) break	d) slim
e) stop	f) pad
g) club	h) step
i) trail	j) walk

3. Add as many suffixes as you can to these words. **Do not double the last letter**, as the stress is not on the final syllable. With a <u>vowel suffix</u>, if the word ends in 'e', remember to remove this first.

a) germinate	b) punish	c) celebrate
d) televise	e) telephone	f) tender
g) orbit	h) decorate	i) accommodate
j) conquer	k) gallop	l) circulate

4. Add as many suffixes as you can to these words. The stress is on the last syllable. If the final vowel sound is short and ends in one consonant, double the last letter when adding a <u>vowel suffix</u>, leave it as it is when adding a <u>consonant suffix</u>.

a) agree	b) inform	c) allow
d) detain	e) commit	f) contain
g) repel	h) picture	i) upset
j) request	k) allot	l) admit
m) compel	n) rebel	o) refer

More work on suffixes can be found on page 76.

ei or ie?

Here is a rhyme you might remember:

i before **e** except after c,
But only when the sound is "ee".

Or we can put it another way:

Use "ei" if it follows a "c", otherwise use "ie".
(ee sounds only).

1. Using this rule, try putting in these missing letters:

a)   bel _ _ ve
b)   th _ _ f
c)   c _ _ ling
d)   gr _ _ f
e)   sh _ _ ld
f)   rel _ _ f
g)   conc _ _ ted
h)   rec _ _ ve
i)   n _ _ ce
j)   pr _ _ st

2. Now try putting the missing letters into this piece.

Thursday was the best day of my whole life.
I rec _ _ ved a call from my n _ _ ce to ask if I'd like to go
and see a band called *Rel _ _ f.*

We took the dog for a br _ _ f walk in the f _ _ lds, and then set off. It was in a town called Duff _ _ ld.

Rel _ _ *f* turned out to be a great band and the theatre was wonderful with a very fancy c _ _ ling. Suddenly, my n _ _ ce said, "I bel _ _ ve the drummer's an old mate of mine."

So after the concert we went backstage.

A security man came running after us, till we explained what we were doing. The drummer was called and said he knew my n _ _ ce. It was a great rel _ _ f!

"Did you think they were th _ _ ves?" he asked.

We chatted for a while, and the drummer said:

"Don't you think we're a brilliant band?"

We laughed.

"I think you're very conc _ _ ted!" my n _ _ ce said, "but you've ach _ _ ved a lot."

He gave us some free tickets for another concert.

Then we set off home. We stopped on the way and had a coffee and a p _ _ ce of cake.

When we got back, the dog had ripped up the TV page.

"You little f _ _ nd!" I said, but I thought it was funny.

here or hear?

These two words sound exactly the same.

'here' means 'this place' and goes with:

here = this place
where = which place
there = that place

'h**ear**' is what you do with your **ear**, or **ears**.
You **hear** sounds.

1. Fill in the gaps, using 'here' or 'hear'.

a)   Can you come ____ please?
b)   I can ____ music.
c)   I think we can get a meal ____.
d)   ____ is your coat.
e)   I'm afraid I can't ____ very well.
f)   I can ___ a dog barking.
g)   The dog is over ____.
h)   You can buy a ticket ____.
i)   I did not ___ that conversation.
j)   You can stay ____ if you wish.
k)   It's less crowded over ____.
l)   Did you ___ what I said?

2. Complete the following:

"I can ____ running water ____," I said to Jack.

"Are you sure?" he replied. "I didn't think there was any water ____."

"Come over ____," I said to him. "If you stand ____, you will ____ it."

is or his?

These two words do sound different, but some local accents pronounce them nearly the same.

is – This little word is part of the verb 'to be'. It is used with he, she, it or a singular noun (naming word).
Examples
He is very angry.
She is not too happy, either.
It is a fine, sunny day.
The table is far too big for this room.

You also use this word with **where**, **there** and **here**. In this case it is actually referring to he, she, it or a singular noun, but this might not be obvious. For example, 'There is only one house down the road' refers to the 'one house'. 'Where is she?' refers to 'she'.

his means 'belonging to him'.
Examples
his name = the name belonging to him.
his house = the house belonging to him.

1. Fill in the gaps, choosing between 'is' and 'his'.

a)   Is that ____ car?
b)   I thought I heard ____ voice.
c)   It ____ raining very hard.
d)   It was ____ idea, not mine.
e)   There ____ only one way to do this.
f)   My son has passed ____ driving test.

g)   It ___ time to go to bed.
h)   The cat ___ on the mat.
i)   ___ anybody there?
j)   I thought I heard ___ voice.
k)   Tom likes ___ new computer.
l)   This road ___ very dangerous.

2. Complete the following:

I'm going to see my brother today. It ___ ___ birthday. He
___ having a party and he ___ inviting all ___ friends and
the family. He hasn't had ___ presents from us yet. He
___ happy to wait till we bring them to ___ party. He ___
going to have a real surprise!

lose or loose?

lose is a verb, or doing word. If you lose something, it is lost. e.g. 'I need to lose weight.'

loose is an adjective, or describing word, meaning 'not tight'. e.g. 'This jumper is very loose.'

1. Fill in the gaps, using 'lose' or 'loose'.

a) It is easy to _____ a key if it is not on a key ring.
b) Children _____ their first teeth.
c) Jack's tooth is very _____.
d) My shoes are too _____.
e) That tennis player is so good he cannot _____.
f) Sometimes we _____ interest in things.
g) Without a map, I might _____ my way.
h) Your dog's collar is very _____.
i) He might _____ it if you don't adjust it.
j) If I have any more time off I could _____ my job.
k) I hope I don't _____ my luggage.
l) That screw has come _____.

2. Complete the following:

I am afraid that I might _____ my watch because the catch is very _____. Once, when I was young, I managed to _____ a lovely bracelet because the catch was _____. My mother says I have always had a tendency to _____ things.

53

Months

Here is a chart showing the number of the month and the order and spelling of the months:

1	January
2	February
3	March
4	April
5	May
6	June
7	July
8	August
9	September
10	October
11	November
12	December

1. Which month comes earlier in the year?

   a) September or March.
   b) March or February.
   c) June or August.
   d) December or October.
   e) July or April.
   f) April or January
   g) May or August.
   h) November or September.
   i) May or July.
   j) November or October.
   k) July or March.
   l) August or October.

2. Which is:

a) The month after March?
b) The month after September?
c) The month before December?
d) The month after June?
e) The first month of the year?
f) The month before October?
g) The month after January?
h) The month after May?
i) The month before July?
j) The last month of the year?
k) The month after September?
l) The month before April?

3. Days in the month

This is a well-known rhyme, or "jingle" to tell us how many days there are in each month.

Thirty days hath bright September,
April, June and dull November,
All the rest have thirty-one,
Apart from February alone,
And that has twenty-eight days clear,
But twenty-nine in each leap year.

Using this information, make a list of the months, showing how many days there are in each.

4. Which month do these dates fall in?

a)   26/2/06
b)   3/9/08
c)   11/7/79
d)   21/12/08
e)   9/8/98
f)   2/3/02
g)   30/4/04
h)   16/5/09
i)   20/10/99
j)   14/6/03

5. Answer these questions

a) What month is your birthday?
b) What month does Christmas fall in?
c) In which month is Bonfire Night?
d) What is the first month of the year?
e) Which month only has 28 days in it?

f) Name one of the hotter months.
g) Name one of the colder months.
h) In which month is the longest day of the year?
i) Which is your favourite month?

Numbers in words

1	one
2	two
3	three
4	four
5	five
6	six
7	seven
8	eight
9	nine
10	ten
11	eleven
12	twelve
13	thirteen
14	fourteen
15	fifteen
16	sixteen
17	seventeen
18	eighteen
19	nineteen
20	twenty

30	thirty
40	forty
50	fifty
60	sixty
70	seventy
80	eighty
90	ninety
100	hundred
1000	thousand

1. Write out these numbers in words.

a)   8
b)   7
c)   14
d)   12
e)   18
f)   23
g)   29
h)   47
i)   61
j)   88
k)   105
l)   398
m)   1872
n)   5029

2. Now write out these in number form.

a)   thirty-three
b)   eighty-nine
c)   five hundred and seventy-four
d)   nine hundred and ninety-nine
e)   two thousand, six hundred and sixty
f)   five thousand, nine hundred and eighty-four
g)   two thousand and five
h)   ten thousand

'of' or 'off'?

Both of these short words have a lot of different meanings. The *sound* of them is quite different, which will help you to choose the right one.

The word, **'of'**, with only one **'f'**, *sounds like* **'ov'**, as if there is a **'v'** in it.

The word **'off'**, with double **'ff'**, sounds the **'ff'**.

Read these sentences, taking careful note of the sound of **'of'** or **'off'**.

of
The machine is out **of** order.
Which day **of** the week is it?
I'd like a glass **of** water.

off
Get **off**!
He ran **off**.
She got **off** the bus.

1. Choose the correct word, 'of' or 'off', and put this in the gaps shown:

a)   I jumped ___ the diving board.
b)   He seemed to have a lot ___ money.
c)   I watch a lot ___ television.
d)   She gave me a bunch ___ flowers.
e)   Come ___ the motorway at the next junction.

f)   I have a lot ____ credit on my phone.
g)   Can you drop me ____ in town, please?
h)   I sent ____ for a new dress.
i)   Can I have a bag ____ sugar, please?
j)   The road turns ____ to the right.
k)   There is a lot ____ choice on the menu today.
l)   A tile has fallen ____ the roof.

Now fill in the missing words:

2. Today was a day ____ surprises. The alarm went ____ a
lot earlier than usual. I had a lot ____ time ahead ____ me,
so I decided I would set ____ to the coast early.
I made a lot ____ sandwiches, and ____ I went.

Take care! People sometimes confuse **of** with **'ve**.

've is short for **have**, and the apostrophe shows that there
are two letters missing:

I should've = 'I should **have**', NOT 'I should of'.
You would've = 'You would **have**', NOT 'You would of'.

Prefixes

Prefixes are parts you can add to the beginning of words, in order to make new words. It works like this:
im + probable = improbable, de + light = delight.

Here is a list of some prefixes which you can add to certain words.

over	under
anti	dis
re	sub
mis	pre
ex	un

1. Add one of the above prefixes to each of these words, and list the new words you have made.

a) historic	f) change
b) marine	g) behave
c) stood	h) take
d) cover	i) fresh
e) septic	j) happy

2. Here is a fuller list of prefixes. Can you think of a word to add to each of these prefixes? Make a list of your own new words.

a) in
b) un
c) im
d) sub

e) mis
f) pre
g) semi
h) en
i) ex
j) re
k) dis
l) de
m) over
n) under
o) anti

qu-

Words in English which begin with 'q' always start with 'qu'. You cannot begin a word with 'q' without using 'qu'. The only exception to this is foreign words or names which we might use in English, for example Iqbal, qat.

1. Fill in the missing words in these sentences, making sure you begin them with 'qu'.

a)   Do you want to ask a _____ ?
b)   The _____ wears a crown for ceremonies.
c)   I can't agree, but I don't want to _____ with you.
d)   There isn't much time so you will have to be _____.
e)   No one was speaking; it was very _____.
f)   The time now is a _____ past six.
g)   In bed you cover yourself with _____.
h)   Ducks make a sound that we call a _____.
i)   You have done _____ well with this.
j)   At the bus stop we form a _____.

2. Make up and write out four separate sentences. In each one, use one of the qu- words above.

quite or quiet?

These two words look very similar.
The two letters at the end are in a different order. Look carefully at them:
quiet   quite
The end sound of these two words is very different.

'quite' has the same pattern at the end, and also the same sound, as these words. Say them, and listen to the end sound:
kite, bite, polite, quite
'quite' means rather, or fairly, and can also mean when something is complete, e.g. 'I'm quite full', 'She's quite tall for her age'.

'quiet' sounds out the '-et' at the end, the same as words such as:
turret, Juliet, diet, quiet
'quiet' means silent, or without noise.

1. Fill in the gaps, using 'quite' or 'quiet'.

a)   The house is _____.
b)   You've done _____ well.
c)   It's _____ a long way from here.
d)   I want some peace and _____.
e)   I wish that dog would be _____.
f)   Our holiday was _____ expensive.
g)   He is a very _____ child.
h)   It's _____ dark outside.
i)   I'm _____ all right, thank you.

j)   It seems _____ now that everyone's gone home.

2. Complete the following, using **quite** or **quiet**:

The garden was very _____, and at first it seemed peaceful. Then I listened, and realised that it was not so _____ at all. The birds were making _____ a lot of noise, and I could hear bees and other insects. I was _____ surprised!

-s, -es plurals

In English spelling, we usually make singular words into plural words simply by adding 's':

one dog, three dogs
one chair, four chairs
one plate, a set of plates
a room, a suite of rooms
a cow, a herd of cows
one table, two tables
the house, a row of houses
one pen, ten pens

If, however, the word ends in a 'hissing' sound (s, ss, x, ch, z, sh) you can't just add an 's' to it. Try saying *matchs, boxs, brushs*!

With these words, you need to add 'es' to make them sound right.

matches   boxes   brushes

1. Make the following singular words into plural, choosing between adding 's' or 'es'.

a) fox__   f) dress__
b) bed__   g) gate__
c) apple__   h) tree__
d) orange__   i) bush__
e) peach__   j) address__
k) church__   p) teacher__

l)	essay__	q)	noodle__
m)	elephant__	r)	buzz__
n)	patch__	s)	television__
o)	letter__	t)	flask__

2. Now re-write the following, changing the words in brackets into plurals:

Today I went to buy my little **(girl)** some new **(shoe)**. The weather was cold, so I thought: New **(coat)**, new **(hat)** and new **(dress)** as well!
In the shoe shop, they asked if we would like to keep the **(box)**.
I decided the best **(coat)** would be nice cosy **(fleece)**.
After the shopping I said, "Let's go to the café for warm **(drink)**, shall we?"
We took so long that we missed two **(bus)**!

Silent e

'Silent e' is an 'e' that we add onto the end of a word to change its sound. Adding 'e' changes a hard (or short) vowel sound into a long (or soft) vowel sound.

This is how it works:

fat + e = fate
pin + e = pine
rob + e = robe
cut + e = cute

Got the idea?

The five vowels are:

a e i o u

It is this sound which changes in the word when we add a 'silent e'.
Look at these:

man: mane
hat: hate
dam: dame
fad: fade
pin: pine
pip: pipe
kit: kite
rid: ride
not: note

rod: rode
dot: dote
pet: Pete
tub: tube

1. Fill in the gaps from the words in brackets:
a)   In winter I always wear a _____. (hat/hate)
b)   I _____ up at six o'clock today. (wok/woke)
c)   A dog makes a good _____. (pet/Pete)
d)   Fir cones grow on a _____ tree. (pin/pine)
e)   The weather is _____ today. (fin/fine)
f)   I like bacon but I _____ eggs. (hat/hate)
g)   It is _____ to go to bed. (Tim/time)
h)   I wrote a short _____. (not/note)
i)   The best fish to eat is _____ . (cod/code)
j)   Children do not play _____ and seek any more. (hid/hide)
k)   I think mice are _____. (cut/cute)
l)   Stir-fry is best cooked in a _____. (wok/woke)

2. Read through this piece of writing. Put a line under all the words that end in a 'silent e':

I was nine when I first rode a bike. My mate Luke gave me his old Raleigh. He had won a new bike as a prize in a contest. I knew Luke would like the chance for us to ride together. So he gave me his old bike.
That old bike became my pride and joy. I put a new tyre on it. I polished the chrome to make it shine. I made it nice. Every time I'd been out for a ride, I gave it a clean. I spent all my spare time on that bike, and gave it lots of care. It was mine, you see.
At first when I rode my bike, it made my legs ache. As time went on they became strong, and soon I could ride a mile or more. Luke and I rode up and down the lane till I knew I was safe to go further away from home.
Then we joined a club so we could get a much longer ride. One day Mr Pike, the man in charge, decided to take

us to Hope Dale Picnic Site. The weather was warm and fine. We went all over the countryside, and rode all day. Then we had a swim in the lake, and lit a fire to bake some potatoes before we came home. I've never known anything taste so good.

When I was twelve I got a bigger, better bike, and again when I left school and got a wage. As I reached each new stage I would change my bike, and move on to another. It's been like that all my life.

I dare not tell you my age, but I still like to ride, come rain or shine. And I still have my old Raleigh bike outside in the shed. People like to come and see it.

I like to see the smile on their face when they stare at my old bike.

Longer words
You can see 'silent e' at the end of many longer words. It always makes the vowel sound 'long'. For example:

mistake   quote
intrude   estimate
invite   enclose
fascinate   electrode
Chinese   outside
elope   telephone
divide   astute

3. What 'silent e' words can *you* think of?

Spelling Method

This section is reproduced from "A Useful Dyslexia Handbook for Adults" by the same author.

Think of between six and ten words that you use regularly and that you **know** you have trouble spelling.

List them here.

1. ....

2. ....

3. ....

4. ....

5. ....

6. ....

7. ....

8. ....

9. ....

10. ....

Ask someone who is good at spelling to check them and list any corrections at the side. Alternatively, you can find them in a dictionary, use your computer spell-checker or a pocket spell-checker.

We are now going to split the words up into chunks.

People like to do this in different ways, depending on how they learn. It is important to split them up in a way that suits you, so you need to try a few different ways.

For example, a lot of people struggle with the word **"information"**.

These are different ways of splitting it, or you might have another way you like better:

in-for-mat-ion

in-form-at-ion

in-for-ma-tion

Or we can try with another word, **"sincerely"**, which causes a lot of problems for people:

sin-cere-ly

s-inc-ere-ly

sinc-er-el-y

since-rely

Get the idea? Now split your own words into chunks.

You need to make a clear list showing first your words, then the way you have split them. It will look something like this:

format	for-mat
television	te-le-vi-sion
business	bus-i-ness
university	uni-ver-sit-y
mathematics	mat-he-mat-ics
necessary	nec-ess-ar-y

This is the basic method for learning your words:

Look, Say, Cover, Write, Check.

...and this is how it's done:

Look at the word and say it at the same time. If you are on your own, do it out loud. Keep doing this until you feel sure of the spelling.
Cover the word up, then try writing it down.
Check to see if you have spelled it correctly.

All of these steps are very important. Do not miss them out.

If you get a word wrong, try again!

Try to spend ten minutes or so each day – more than once if you wish – on this activity. If you are feeling tired with it, put it away and come back later.

At the end of a week, ask someone to test you on the spellings.

If you have got them right, try using each one in a sentence. If you have not yet learned a word, it can simply go into a new list.

You are now ready for a fresh list of spellings, but keep on using the ones you have learned!

Suffixes

Suffixes are parts you can add to the end of words, in order to make new words. As an example, here is a list of some suffixes:

-ance	-ly
-less	-able
-ful	-er
-ness	-ship
-y	-ment

1. Add one of the above suffixes to each of these words. List the new words you have made.

a) rain	f) friend
b) garden	g) attend
c) care	h) hope
d) kind	i) sure
e) break	j) pay

Sometimes, when you add a suffix, you have to change the last letter of the word you are adding it to. These are the rules:

<u>Words with short vowel sounds ending in one consonant</u>
First, let us look at words with a **short vowel sound ending in one consonant**, such as top, cat.

If you are adding a consonant suffix (a suffix beginning with a consonant), the word stays the same, for example:

mad + ness = madness
mad + ly = madly

If you are adding a vowel suffix (a suffix beginning with a vowel), you double the last letter, for example:
trek + er = trekker
trek + ing = trekking

N.B. The above rule does not apply to words ending in x.

Words with short vowel sounds ending in two consonants
Now let's look at words with a **short vowel sound ending in two consonants**, such as 'soft'. For these, the word stays the same for any suffix you are adding. For example:

soft + ly = softly
soft + ness = softness
soft + er = softer

Words ending in y
Next we have words **ending in a 'y'**. For these words you change the 'y' to 'i' when you add any suffix. For example:

tidy + er = tidier
tidy + ly = tidily
tidy + ness = tidiness

cosy + er = cosier
cosy + ly = cosily
cosy + ness = cosiness

Words with a long vowel sound in the final syllable
Finally, let us take a look at words **with a long vowel sound in the final syllable**. If this is created by using a 'silent e', for example 'hope', you will need to remove the 'silent e' before adding a vowel suffix. If you are adding a consonant suffix, leave the word as it is. For example:

hope + ing = hoping
hope + ful = hopeful

For words with a long vowel sound NOT created by using a 'silent e', just add the suffix. For example:

pain + ful = painful
pain + less = painless
pain + ed = pained

2. Add as many different suffixes as you can to these words, following the rules:

a) post
b) care
c) fear
d) pave

e) stop
f) look
g) regret
h) bet

i) govern
j) improve
k) pot
l) roast

m) step
n) pass
o) shop
p) forget

Syllables

Syllables are units of sound in words. For example, the word 'dandelion' has four syllables, **dan-de-li-on**.

1. How many syllables are there in:

- Your first name?
- Your second name?
- My first name?
- My second name?

2. Got the idea? Write down how many syllables there are in each of these words:

a)   London
b)   college
c)   computer
d)   Leeds
e)   Denmark
f)   Manchester
g)   carpet
h)   table
i)   telephone
j)   me
k)   after
l)   like
m)   chocolate
n)   information
o)   essay
p)   classroom
q)   refectory

r) exam
s) paper
t) university

there, their or they're?

These are difficult to remember, and you will need to keep checking to see that you have used the correct word.

<u>there</u>
It means "that place". For example:
I live over **there**.
There is a tree in my garden.
There she goes.
It goes with:
here = this place
where = what place
there = that place

<u>their</u>
It means "belonging to them". For example:
Their house = The house belonging to them.
This is **their** son = This is the son belonging to them.

<u>they're</u>
It is short for "they are", and the apostrophe shows that the 'a' is missing. For example:
They're leaving = They are leaving.
I can see that **they're** not very good = I can see that they are not very good.

Fill in the gaps with "there", "their" or "they're".

1.
a) The college is over _____.
b) _____ are plenty of spaces for parking.
c) Craig and Narina are eating _____ dinner.
d) _____ taking an exam today.
e) _____ is no water in the kettle, and _____ are no tea-bags.
f) Sheep always know _____ own lambs.
g) _____ is a telephone call for you.
h) I left my book over _____.
i) Students have _____ own lockers.
j) _____ very lucky to have a locker each.
k) Last night _____ was a good programme on TV.
l) _____ going to repeat it on Sunday.

2.
Most people these days have _____ own personal computer. This means that _____ able to use the Internet and have _____ own e-mail address. They can do _____ shopping, organise _____ money, type _____ own letters and do many other wonderful things. The world is changing, but _____ are some people who think that life was better before the days of the PC. They believe that _____ work was much simpler, and that _____ was a slower pace to life.

3.
_____ was no need for her to go out that day. _____ was plenty of food in the house, and _____ were no children to pick up from school. They were still with _____ grandparents. _____ were just the two of them. Tonight was _____ last chance.

they or there?

they = people or things. For example:

They are going on holiday next week.
I think **they** are on the shelf.
I wonder if **they** will come?

The **sound** of this word rhymes with:

say	day
may	pay
lay	ray
bay	hay
stay	pray

Say each of these words in turn.
Now say **'they'**. Look at the word and say it, then write it down:

there = 'place'. **There** is, **there** are, over **there**. For example:

I think I left them over **there**.
There is a spider in the bath.
There were only two books on the table.
There was just me.
Can you stand over **there**, please?

The **sound** of this word rhymes with:

bare	care
mare	dare
rare	stare

air   fair
hair   pair

Say each of these words in turn.
Now say **'there'**. Look at the word and say it. Then write it down.

Put **they** or **there** into the gaps. Then read the passages, to check that you have chosen the right word.

1.
Last week my cat had kittens. _____ were five altogether. The mother cat carried them all into the airing cupboard because she knew _____ were safe and warm in _____. _____ were all black and white, like their mother. When _____ are six weeks old I shall have to find homes for them. I will make sure _____ go to a very good home. I'm going to keep one, so _____ will only be four homes to find.

2.
_____ is an interesting family who live in that house over _____. _____ have twins and triplets. The twins are boys. _____ are ten years old. _____ are identical. It's hard to tell who _____ are. _____ go everywhere together, and _____ do everything together. Then _____ are the triplets. _____ all have ginger hair, and _____ all look alike too. _____ are seven, and _____ are all girls. Their personalities seem different. Sometimes I can hear them when _____ are falling out with each other. But afterwards _____ make friends again. _____ are all nice children.

3.
I'm sure I left my keys over _____, but _____ seem to be missing. _____ are four keys on the bunch, and _____ is a blue tag on the key-ring. _____ are the keys to my car and my house, so I need to find them. If

you find them over _____, could you let me know? Or _____ can be left with Reception. _____ is always someone _____.

to, two or too?

to, **two** and **too** have almost the same sound, but their meanings are different. You will need to check the meaning so that you can decide which one to use.

to = towards something. For example:
I am going **to** the door.
Jack is going **to** take his exam.
It is time **to** go.

two = number 2. For example:
I have **two** dogs.
I'd like **two** bottles of milk, please.

Too = 'also' or 'more than there should be'. For example:
Jan is coming **too**.
I have a dog **too**.
There is **too** much milk in my tea.
That car is far **too** much money.

1. Fill the gaps with 'to', 'two' or 'too'.

a)   She is going ___ town.
b)   I have ___ children.
c)   It's ___ hot in here.
d)   I like cooking ___.
e)   It's ___ o'clock.
f)   I am going ___ the dentist.
g)   My little boy is ___ years old.
h)   I have a daughter ___.
i)   You work ___ hard.

j)   It's ___ late ___ go ___ the shop.
k)   I need ___ take your photo.
l)   There are ___ many people in the car.
m)   I need ___ go ___ bed.
n)   I have one or ___ books you might like.
o)   This tee-shirt is far ___ small.
p)   My coffee is ___ hot.
q)   I asked for ___ cups of tea.

2. Complete the following, using **to**, **two** or **too**.

I am going ___ get up early tomorrow. I have ___ interesting things ___ do. First, I am going ___ a show. It starts at ___ o'clock. My sister is coming ___. She has ___ dogs in the show.
This evening I am going with ___ friends ___ see a local band. We are going with ___ other people who I don't know. We are going in their car. Mine is ___ small. I hope the music isn't ___ loud!

Vowels

The vowels are:
a e i o u

These are important because they are all "open mouth" sounds, and link the other letters.

The other letters are called "consonants".

1. Can you find the vowels in these words?

a)   blackbird
b)   shopping
c)   marathon
d)   London
e)   college
f)   telephone
g)   encourage
h)   caravan
i)   sister
j)   brother
k)   swimming
l)   running
m)   carpet
n)   newspaper
o)   photograph
p)   employment
q)   Helen
r)   Jonathon
s)   touring
t)   emergency

u)   Colorado

Each of the vowels makes two different sounds. These are:

The **soft** (long) sound.
The **hard** (short) sound.

The soft (long) sound is the name of the letter.
The hard (short) sound is the sound the letter makes.

<u>Examples</u>	<u>a</u>	<u>e</u>	i	<u>o</u>	<u>u</u>
Soft sound	made	Pete	fine	rope	tube
Hard sound	man	pet	bin	pot	but

2. Look at these words. Decide if the vowel sound underlined is **short**, or **long**. Sometimes two vowels are used together.

a) cup
b) paper
c) tea
d) sky
e) shape
f) John
g) sweet
h) waste
i) spot
j) post
k) pillow
l) bottle
m) computer
n) butter
o) metal
p) rabbit
q) tube
r) field
s) beetle
t) college

were, we're or where?

People often have trouble confusing these words.

were – This word is the past tense of 'are', from the verb 'to be'. It goes with 'we', 'you' and 'they'. It is also used with **here**, **where** and **there**.
Examples
We were watching a good TV programme.
I believe you were at the concert. Were you at the concert?
They were trying to get to the top of the mountain.
There were three children in the car.

we're is short for we are. The apostrophe shows that there is a missing letter, 'a'.
Examples
We're leaving now. = We **a**re leaving now.
We're very pleased about that. = We **a**re very pleased about that.

where means 'which place'. It goes with here (this place) and there (that place).
w**here**
t**here**
 here
Examples
Where are you going?
I'm going where you will never find me.
Do you know where she parked the car?

1. Fill in the gaps, using were, we're or where:

a) I don't know _____ to look.
b) _____ going on holiday tomorrow.
c) _____ did you put the newspaper?
d) _____ there is life, there is hope.
e) There _____ only two places left.
f) When you _____ a small child, you used to say funny things.
g) I'm not sure if _____ supposed to be doing this.
h) I don't know _____ you live.
i) At one time there _____ fish in this river.
j) Next week _____ having a party outside in the garden.
k) _____ inviting all the neighbours.
l) Please put this _____ it will be safe.
m) We _____ hoping that you would be able to come to dinner.
n) I can't see _____ I'm going.
o) _____ the best people for the job.

2. Complete the following, using **were, we're** or **where**:

"_____ are we going?" I asked.
"_____ going on a mystery tour," my sister replied.
"I thought we _____ going to London."
She laughed.
"Yes, I know you thought you _____ going to London!"
"Don't you know _____ the mystery tour is going?"
"No. _____ having a surprise."

whose or who's?

These two words are easily confused by people, as the sound is the same.

whose = belonging to who
Examples
Whose is that coat?
It depends whose house we are going to.

who's = *who is,* or *who has*

who is
The apostrophe shows that a letter is missing, in this case 'i'.
Examples
Who's that over there? = Who **is** that over there?
I don't know who's going and who is not. = I don't know who **is** going and who is not.

who has
The apostrophe shows that two letters are missing, in this case 'ha'.
Examples
Who's done that? = Who **has** done that?
Who's been to France? = Who **has** been to France?

1. Fill in the gaps, using **whose** or **who's**. If in doubt, try 'who is' or 'who has' in the gap first, to see if it makes sense or not.

a)   I don't know _____ desk this is.

b)   _____ done that?
c)   _____ a clever girl, then?
d)   _____ car shall we go in?
e)   _____ that man over there?
f)   Do you know _____ turn it is?
g)   We need to find out _____ got a ticket.
h)   I need to know _____ done this.
i)   _____ next, please?
j)   Please let me know _____ team you are in.
k)   _____ the best person for the job?
l)   _____ been eating my porridge?
m)   _____ working on that computer?
n)   I'm not sure _____ bag that is.
o)   I'll never know _____ done this.

2. Complete the following, using **whose** or **who's**:

"_____ written this?" I asked.
"I don't know _____ writing that is," Ella replied, "but I
know _____ just bought a pen with purple ink!"
"_____ that?" I queried.
"The same person _____ got a pad of pink paper."
"_____ pen is it?" I persisted, "and _____ paper is it?"
"Look over there," Ella said, "and you'll soon know _____
writing it is."

Words that look like 'though'

though   through   thought   thorough

These words look very similar to each other, and are very easy to confuse.

They all begin with 'th' and have 'ough' in them. Let's look at each of them separately.

though = however or 'despite the fact that'
This word rhymes with 'no'. Look at it and think of the way you say it. It begins with 'th', followed by 'ough' - which in this type of word says a long 'oh'. (th+oh)

Here are some more that follow the same pattern:

though
dough
although

Say the words. Can you hear the same sound?

through = going in at one side and out at the other
This word looks almost the same, but there is an 'r' after the 'th', and the 'ough' in this word says 'oo'. Think of the different sounds in the word. (th+r+oo) Say the word.
This word has its own pattern and sound.

thought = past tense of think, or an idea

This word looks almost the same as 'though' except that it has a 't' at the end. The 'ough' in this word says 'or'. Think of the different sounds in this word. (th+or+t)

Here are some more that follow the same pattern:
thought
bought
ought
nought

Say the words. Can you hear the same sound?

thorough = completely and carefully
This word is longer than the others, and has an extra sound. It has two syllables instead of one. It sounds like 'thurra', which we can split up like this: 'th-u-rr-a'. Try saying it. It has the same sound as 'borough' in many place names:

thorough
borough
Scarborough
Littleborough
Boroughbridge

Can you hear the same sound?

though
What does this word mean? Say the word. Write two sentences, each containing the word 'though'.

....
....
....
....

through

What does this word mean? Say the word. Write two sentences, each containing the word 'through'.

....

....

....

....

thought

What does this word mean? Say the word. Write two sentences, each containing the word 'thought'.

....

....

....

....

thorough

What does this word mean? Say the word. Write two sentences, each containing the word 'thorough'.

....

....

....

....

1. Now put the missing word into these sentences. Is it:

though   through   thought   thorough   ?

a) I went .... the door, and closed it behind me.

b) Have you .... about what you want to do?

c) I .... I might go on holiday.

d) The tutor's marking was very ....

e) I'd like to work in a big company, ... there's always my dad's business which I .... I could try.

f) I had a very strange .... this morning.

g) I've worked .... all the questions she set me.

h) He didn't win a prize, even .... his entry was very good.

i) She's a .... worker.

j) It was .... my own fault that I missed the bus.

2. Complete the following, using **though, through, thought** or **thorough**:

It was a difficult and, I _____, a very interesting situation. I _____ about it for a long time. I wanted to be very _____. Then I realised that I needed to talk it _____ with someone. I _____ about who could help me, _____ deep down I knew I would have to sort it out myself.

'y' plurals

Singular = one, e.g. a dog, the house, one apple.
Plural = more than one, e.g. two dogs, four houses, some apples.

If a noun (name word) ends in 'y', there are two ways of making into a plural. Here is the rule:

Look at the letter **before** the 'y'.

If the letter before the 'y' is a vowel (**a e i o u**), simply add 's'.

e.g. one donk**e**y, six donkeys.

If the letter before the 'y' is a consonant (not a vowel), drop the 'y' and add '-ies'.

e.g. a ba**b**y, two babies.

1. Make these singular words into plurals:

a) A ferry, two _____
b) The lorry, a fleet of _____
c) One boy, three _____
d) A red jelly, a choice of _____
e) One day, seven _____
f) A calamity, a series of _____
g) A political party, all the political _____
h) One guy, two _____
i) A motorway, Britain's _____

j)   A good hobby, some good _____

2. Louise has left a note for Tom, who has kindly offered to go to the supermarket. Following the rules, turn all the singular words in brackets into plurals.

4 Cornish (pasty)
Pkt baps for bacon (butty)
4 Danish (pastry)
4 gingerbread (teddy)
2 vegetable (curry)
2 Cadbury's Milk (Tray)
6 children's (lolly)
Pkt toffee (candy)
Some little (toy) for the kids.
2 Matthews' frozen (turkey)
Pkt frozen French (fry)
2 orange (jelly)
Bottle cocktail (cherry)
Box paper (hanky)
Pack disposable (nappy)
2 different (honey)
Punnet (strawberry)
4 Size C (battery)
2 new (key) cut at kiosk

P.S. Park next to where the (trolley) are – that's where the bottle bank is so you can throw away the (empty). And could you find a DVD with children's (story) on it please? Thanks.

your or you're?

your always means 'belonging to you'.
Examples
Have you got your key? = Have you got 'the key belonging to you'?
It's your birthday tomorrow = It's the 'birthday belonging to you' tomorrow.
Your mobile phone is ringing = The 'mobile phone belonging to you' is ringing.

you're always means 'you are'.
The apostrophe shows that there is a missing letter, 'a'.
Examples
You're my best friend. = You are my best friend.
You're going the wrong way. = You are going the wrong way.

1. Fill in the gaps, using, 'your' or 'you're'.

a)   Is that _____ car?
b)   Please turn _____ computer off.
c)   I think _____ a wonderful person.
d)   What is _____ name?
e)   _____ quite right about that.
f)   I think I know _____ sister.
g)   _____ doing really well with that.
h)   Is this _____ coat?
i)   _____ on the wrong train!
j)   Do you know where _____ going?
k)   Shall we go to _____ house?
l)   It was _____ idea.

2. Complete the following, using **your** or **you're**.

Now that _____ getting older, I would like to tell you about _____ grandfather. _____ very like him. _____ hair is exactly the same colour as his was, and _____ eyes too. _____ also very similar in _____ looks. I see _____ interested in animals, just as he was. I sometimes wonder if _____ going to be a vet, too, and make _____ living from it like _____ grandfather did. I know you will do _____ best, whatever _____ choice. It's the way _____ made.

ANSWERS

Alphabetical order,

1.   (Self-check)

2.
a)
apple
banana
cherry
lemon
orange
pear
strawberry
tangerine.

b)
cat
dog
elephant
frog
giraffe
horse
mouse
ostrich
rat
tiger.

c)
Ann
Ben
Callum

Jane
Leanne
Shaheen
Taz
Zoe

d)
Anderson
Cliffe
Davis
Everett
Jones
Kauser
Lenski
McDonald
Smith
Wilson

3.
a)
America
Austria
England
Finland
France
Germany
Iceland
Ireland

b)
Dining tables
Dinner sets
DIY
Football boots
Fragrances
Fridges
Schoolwear
Shoes

Shower curtain
Sportswear

4.
a)
cappuccino
cocoa
coffee
cola
Cordial
Milk
Tea
Water

b)
Bradford
Bridgend
Bridgwater
Chester
Chesterfield
Huddersfield
Hull
Thetford
Thirsk

5.
Alderson, G
Ali, M
Anderson, G
Burley, W
Chan, P
Jacks, S
Jackson, O
Jackson, P
Johnson, P
Jones, K
McDonald A
MacDonald, J

Mackie, F
Mackintosh, G
Moss, J
Oakes, S
Oates, S
Sutton, D
Sutton, M
Walton, R

a or an

1.
a)   **a** letter
b)   **an** owl
c)   **a** chair
d)   **a** pen
e)   **an** orange
f)   **a** banana
g)   **a** horse
h)   **a** map
i)   **an** honest man
j)   **an** hour or two
k)   **a** half-hour
l)   **a** hopeful letter

2.
Last week I went to **a** different supermarket for **a** change.
I found **an** empty parking space straight away. Then I got
a trolley. I was pleased to find that there was **a** small one,
which is better for **a** person like me who doesn't need **a** lot
of things.
I got **a** lettuce, **a** cucumber and **an** onion to make **a** salad.
Then I filled **a** bag with carrots. I decided I wanted **an**
apple, so I got **a** few.
I went to get **a** loaf of bread and saw that I could get **a** hot
pie. I also got **a** bottle of milk and **a** packet of butter, which
was **a** low-fat type. I was pleased to see **a** lot of meals
with **a** one-person sized helping.

Then I noticed it was raining, so I bought **an** umbrella. On the way out I saw I could get **a** magazine and **a** newspaper. I had **a** look at my watch, and saw I'd been **an** hour in there. That was **a** real surprise!

affect or effect

1.
a) Taking too much time off work could **affect** your job.
b) Watching a sad film always has a bad **effect** on me.
c) Sad films **affect** me too.
d) This medication has one very strong side **effect**.
e) The holiday has had a remarkable **effect** on her.
f) Too much sun can **affect** your skin.
g) Sun and rain together create a beautiful **effect** called a rainbow.
h) Bright lights do **affect** me.
i) I do not allow bad weather to **affect** me.
j) The theatre company used green lighting to create an eerie **effect**.

2.
I had a big meal late last night which **affected** me badly. The **effect** of it was terrible. I could not sleep, and when I did drop off, I had vivid dreams with a cinema-type **effect**. I told my friend how I had been **affected**. She told me that too much food late at night always **affects** her, too.

overdose did miolo

-al, -el or –le

a) I'm going to see my auntie and **uncle** next week.
b) Shake the liquid, and then wait for it to **settle** down.

c)   You might not agree with each other, but please try not to **quarrel**.
d)   A **camel** is a creature with one or two humps which lives in the desert.
e)   The coloured part of a flower is called the **petal**.
f)   My sister collects **model** cars.
g)   My dog is very soft and **gentle**.
h)   I've got toothache so I will make a **dental** appointment.
i)   Shall I fill the **kettle** and we can have a hot drink?
j)   Close the door please, using the **handle**.
k)   A **thistle** is a very prickly plant.
l)   Many clocks have a **digital** display.

Apostrophe s, verb s or plural s (Also other uses of the apostrophe)

1.
a)   I will buy the **meals**.
b)   She is going to look at the **rooms**.
c)   I eat **cereals** every day.
d)   Which **carpets** do you like best?
e)   Which **jobs** are you interested in?
f)   I've hurt my **legs**.
g)   Remember to pull out the **plugs**.
h)   Don't forget to pick up the **keys**.
i)   They sat in the shade of the **trees**.
j)   Can you switch on the **lights**, please?

2.
a)   That car **needs** a good wash.
b)   Jack **speaks** a different language.
c)   The shop **closes/shuts** at half past nine.
d)   Ashley **takes** his dog for a walk every day.
e)   Arshad **eats** a chocolate bar every morning.
f)   Karen **drinks** a lot of coffee.

g)   He always **makes** us laugh.

h)   She **drives** the car slowly.

i)   The telephone **rings** all the time.

j)   Oliver always **eats** a big breakfast.

3.

a)   They searched the **lists** to find the **man's** name.

b)   We took **boots**, **coats**, **hats** and thick **socks** for our **week's** holiday.

c)   Kevin always **sulks** when he **sees** his **brother's** car.

d)   Our **cat** sleeps in the **dog's** basket.

e)   There is **always** the **tutor's** book which **tells** us the **answers**.

f)   He **says** he **knows** the **children's names**.

g)   **Jessica's** mum **likes carrots**, **peas** and **cabbage.**

h)   He never **reads yesterday's newspapers.**

i)   Tim **plays** the piano but never touches his **sister's** guitar.

j)   The phone **rings** all the time in **Tom's** office.

4.

a)   You will never learn.

b)   I know he will win.

c)   There is only a day left.

d)   I cannot come.

e)   That is life.

f)   He will not do as he is told.

g)   I will ring you.

h)   I did not know that.

i)   He does not know either.

j)   I would not go into town if I were you.

k)   She could not climb the stairs.

l)   I shall not ring her.

m)   What is the title of that book?

n)   There will never be another like it.

as or has

1.
a)   He **has** been to the cinema with me.
b)   The film was very good, **as** we expected.
c)   My brother Jack **has** a very good MP3 player.
d)   He **has** lived there for a very long time.
e)   I saw the castle **as** we drove past.
f)   There **has** never been a better time.
g)   Laura **has** a very good job.
h)   He was there **as** quick **as** a flash.
i)   He **has** given me a lovely present.
j)   Could I have some more cake, please, **as** it's my birthday?

2.
As there **has** been very little interest in the soup, it **has** been decided to take this off the canteen menu. It **has** also been noted that there are not **as** many people buying salad **as** last year, so the manager **has** made the decision to serve this **as** a side dish. Nothing else **has** been changed.

b or d

1.

	Word	Correct? YES or NO	Should be:
a)	duddles	**NO**	**bubbles**
b)	dabble	**YES**	
c)	Brabford	**NO**	**Bradford**
d)	robbed	**YES**	
e)	bramdles	**NO**	**brambles**
f)	candle	**YES**	
g)	fadulous	**NO**	**fabulous**
h)	Dudlin	**NO**	**Dublin**
i)	soba water	**NO**	**soda water**
k)	cupdoard	**NO**	**cupboard**
l)	stadle	**NO**	**stable**
m)	cubble	**NO**	**cuddle**

2.
a)   ground
b)   before
c)   debt
d)   candle
e)   baby
f)   rosebud
g)   stopped
h)   tablet
i)   badger
j)   bedroom

Compound words
1.
a)   light   house
b)   rail   way
c)   butter   fly

d)   water   proof
e)   table   cloth
f)   wind   screen
g)   no   body
h)   Ice   land
i)   news   paper
j)   friend   ship
k)   motor   way
l)   pine   apple
m)   black   mail
n)   break   fast
o)   ear   wig
p)   car   pet
q)   butter   cup
r)   tap   pet
s)   tooth   ache
t)   fork   lift

insect

n. arandren or tije rebe

earwig

butter cup   bright yellow wildflower
n. boton de oro

tappet   n. mecánica vástago, rogvé

forklift   n. Toro, camehilla elevadora, ngwtortoenga

2.
a)   windscreen
b)   countryside
c)   blackbird
d)   database   — n. base de datos
e)   headquarters
f)   outline   — v deline ah, resumir = summarize
g)   internet
h)   clockwise   — adv en sentido horario
i)   cupboard
j)   horseshoe   — n. herradura /hɔ:sʃuɪ/
k)   bathroom
l)   overtake   — v adelantar
m)   photograph
n)   sometimes

3.
a)   understand
b)   eyeball   glbs oaln

111

c)	toothpaste
d)	nowhere (or nothing)
e)	something (or somewhere)
f)	hopeless
g)	spreadsheet
h)	gooseberry
i)	foolproof
j)	butterfly
k)	grandfather
l)	friendship
m)	overload
n)	outlook

4.
a)	Blackpool
b)	Cornwall
c)	Wakefield
d)	Newcastle
e)	Oldham
f)	Yorkshire

5. (Suggestions)
a)	lifeboat, lifebelt
b)	grandmother,		grandfather,		grandson,
	granddaughter, grandma, granddad
c)	grapefruit
d)	strawberry
e)	peacock, peahen, peanut
f)	sunshine, sunshade, suntan, sunrise, sunset
g)	hedgehog
h)	tablecloth, tablespoon, tablemat
i)	greenhouse, greenfly
j)	headline, headboard, headmaster
k)	seaside, seagull,
l)	fireguard, fireman
m)	railway, railtrack, railroad
n)	cupboard
o)	nightdress, nightgown, nightcap

112

p)   woodland, woodworm
q)   moonlight
r)   staircase, stairway

Consonants

a) window
b) tooth, teeth
c) television
d) pencil
e) bottle, battle
f) basket
g) light
h) dinner
i) kitten
j) banana
k) tablet
l) ladybird
m) sugar
n) music
o) wagon
p) supermarket
q) matches
r) peacock
s) football

Double trouble

1.
a)   hope, hopeful, hopeless
b)   dim, dimness, dimly
c)   glad, gladness, gladly
d)   fat, fatness, fatty
e)   kind, kindness, kindly
f)   bad, badness, badly
g)   short, shortness, shortly
h)   joy, joyful, joyless

i) mad, madness, madly
j) tact, tactless, tactful

2.
a) pat, patter, patted, patting
b) bet, better, betted, betting
c) break, breaking, breakable
d) slim, slimmer, slimmed, slimming
e) stop, stopper, stopping, stopped, stoppable
f) pad, padded, padding,
g) club, clubbed, clubber, clubbing
h) step, stepped, stepping
i) trail, trailer, trailed, trailing
j) walk, walked, walking

3.
a) germinate, germinates, germinating, germinated
b) punish, punishes, punished, punishing, punishable
c) celebrate, celebrates, celebrated, celebrating, celebration
d) televise, televised, televising, television
e) telephone, telephones, telephoned, telephoning
f) tender, tenders, tendered, tendering, tenderly, tenderness
g) orbit, orbits, orbiting, orbited
h) decorate, decorates, decorating, decorated, decoration
i) accommodate, accommodates, accommodated, accommodating, accommodation
j) conquer, conquers, conquering, conquered, conqueror
k) gallop, gallops, galloped, galloping
l) circulate, circulates, circulated, circulating, circulation

4.
a) agree, agrees, agreed, agreeing, agreeable
b) inform, informs, informed, informing,

c) allow, allows, allowed, allowing, allowable
d) detain, detains, detained, detaining, detainee
e) commit, commits, committing, committed, commitment
f) contain, container, contained
g) repel, rebels, repelled, repelling
h) picture, pictures, picturing, pictured
i) upset, upsets, upsetting
j) request, requests, requesting, requested
k) allot, allots, allotting, allotted, allotment
l) admit, admits, admitted, admitting, admittance
m) compel, compels, compelling, compelled
n) rebel, rebels, rebelling, rebelled, rebellious
o) refer, refers, referring, referred, reference

ei or ie

1.
a) believe
b) thief
c) ceiling
d) grief
e) shield
f) relief
g) conceited
h) receive
i) niece
j) priest

2.
Thursday was the best day of my whole life.
I received a call from my niece to ask if I'd like to go and
see a band called *Relief*.
We took the dog for a brief walk in the fields, and then
set off. It was in a town called Duffield.

Relief turned out to be a great band and the theatre was wonderful with a very fancy ceiling. Suddenly, my niece said, "I believe the drummer's an old mate of mine."

So after the concert we went backstage.

A security man came running after us, till we explained what we were doing. The drummer was called and said he knew my niece. It was a great relief!

"Did you think they were thieves?" he asked.

We chatted for a while, and the drummer said:

"Don't you think we're a brilliant band?"

We laughed.

"I think you're very conceited!" my niece said, "but you've achieved a lot."

He gave us some free tickets for another concert.

Then we set off home. We stopped on the way and had a coffee and a piece of cake.

When we got back, the dog had ripped up the TV page.

"You little fiend!" I said, but I thought it was funny.

here or hear

1.
a)   Can you come **here** please?
b)   I can **hear** music.
c)   I think we can get a meal **here**.
d)   **Here** is your coat.
e)   I'm afraid I can't **hear** very well.
f)   I can **hear** a dog barking.
g)   The dog is over **here**.
h)   You can buy a ticket **here**.
i)   I did not **hear** that conversation.
j)   You can stay **here** if you wish.
k)   It's less crowded over **here**.
l)   Did you **hear** what I said?

2.
"I can **hear** running water **here**," I said to Jack.

"Are you sure?" he replied. "I didn't think there was any water **here**."
"Come over **here**," I said to him. "If you stand **here**, you will **hear** it."

is or his

1.
a)   Is that **his** car?
b)   I thought I heard **his** voice.
c)   It **is** raining very hard.
d)   It was **his** idea, not mine.
e)   There **is** only one way to do this.
f)   My son has passed **his** driving test.
g)   It **is** time to go to bed.
h)   The cat **is** on the mat.
i)   **Is** anybody there?
j)   I thought I heard **his** voice.
k)   Tom likes **his** new computer.
l)   This road **is** very dangerous.

2.
I'm going to see my brother today. It **is his** birthday. He **is** having a party and he **is** inviting all **his** friends and the family. He hasn't had **his** presents from us yet. He **is** happy to wait till we bring them to **his** party. He **is** going to have a real surprise!

lose or loose

1.
a)   It is easy to **lose** a key if it is not on a key ring.
b)   Children **lose** their first teeth.
c)   Jack's tooth is very **loose**.
d)   My shoes are too **loose**.
e)   That tennis player is so good he cannot **lose**.
f)   Sometimes we **lose** interest in things.

g)   Without a map, I might **lose** my way.
h)   Your dog's collar is very **loose**.
i)   He might **lose** it if you don't adjust it.
j)   If I have any more time off I could **lose** my job.
k)   I hope I don't **lose** my luggage.
l)   That screw has come **loose**.

2. Complete the following:
I am afraid that I might **lose** my watch because the catch is very **loose**. Once, when I was young, I managed to **lose** a lovely bracelet because the catch was **loose**.
My mother says I have always had a tendency to **lose** things.

Months

1.
a)	March	g) May
b)	February	h) September
c)	June	i) May
d)	October	j) October
e)	April	k) March
f)	January	l) August

2.
a)	April	e) January
b)	October	f) September
c)	November	g) February
d)	July	h) June
i)	January	k) October
j)	December	l) March

3.
January	31	July	31
February	28 (29 leap year)	August	31
March	31	September	30
April	30	October	31
May	31	November	30

June   30   December   31

4.
a)   February
b)   September
c)   July
d)   December
e)   August
f)   March
g)   April
h)   May
i)   October
j)   June

5.
a)   (Various)
b)   December
c)   November
d)   January
e)   February
f)   June/July/August
g)   December/January/February
h)   June
i)   (Various)

Numbers in words

1.
a)   eight
b)   seven
c)   fourteen
d)   twelve
e)   eighteen
f)   twenty-three
g)   twenty-nine
h)   forty-seven

i)   sixty-one
j)   eighty-eight
k)   one hundred and five
l)   three hundred and ninety-eight
m)   one thousand, eight hundred and seventy-two
n)   five thousand and twenty-nine

2.
a)   33
b)   89
c)   574
d)   999
e)   2660
f)   5984
g)   2005
h)   10,000

of or off

1.
a)   I jumped **off** the diving board.
b)   He seemed to have a lot **of** money.
c)   I watch a lot **of** television.
d)   She gave me a bunch **of** flowers.
e)   Come **off** the motorway at the next junction.
f)   I have a lot **of** credit on my phone.
g)   Can you drop me **off** in town, please?
h)   I sent **off** for a new dress.
i)   Can I have a bag **of** sugar, please?
j)   The road turns **off** to the right.
k)   There is a lot **of** choice on the menu today.
l)   A tile has fallen **off** the roof.

2. Today was a day **of** surprises. The alarm went **off** a lot earlier than usual. I had a lot **of** time ahead **of** me, so I decided I would set **off** to the coast early.
I made a lot **of** sandwiches, and **off** I went.

Prefixes

1.
a)   **pre**historic
b)   **sub**marine
c)   **under**stood
d)   **dis**cover
e)   **anti**septic
f)   **ex**change
g)   **mis**behave
h)   **over**take
j)   **re**fresh
k)   **un**happy

2.
(Self-check)

qu
1.
a)   Do you want to ask a **question**?
b)   The **queen** wears a crown for ceremonies.
c)   I can't agree, but I don't want to **quarrel** with you.
d)   There isn't much time so you will have to be **quick**.
e)   No one was speaking; it was very **quiet**.
f)   The time now is a **quarter** past six.
g)   In bed you cover yourself with **quilt**.
h)   Ducks make a sound that we call a **quack**.
i)   You have done **quite** well with this.
j)   At the bus stop we form a **queue**.

2.
(Self-check)

quite or quiet,
1.
a)   The house is **quiet**.
b)   You've done **quite** well.

c) It's **quite** a long way from here.
d) I want some peace and **quiet**.
e) I wish that dog would be **quiet**.
f) Our holiday was **quite** expensive.
g) He is a very **quiet** child.
h) It's **quite** dark outside.
i) I'm **quite** all right, thank you.
j) It seems **quiet** now that everyone's gone home.

2.

The garden was very **quiet**, and at first it seemed peaceful. Then I listened, and realised that it was not so **quiet** at all. The birds were making **quite** a lot of noise, and I could hear bees and other insects. I was **quite** surprised!

-s, -es plurals

1.

a) fox**es**
b) bed**s**
c) apple**s**
d) orange**s**
e) peach**es**
f) dress**es**
g) gate**s**
h) tree**s**
i) bush**es**
j) address**es**

k) church**es**
l) essay**s**
m) elephant**s**
n) patch**es**
o) letter**s**
p) teacher**s**
q) noodle**s**
r) buzz**es**
s) television**s**
t) flask**s**

2.

Today I went to buy my little **girls** some new **shoes**. The weather was cold, so I thought: New **coats**, new **hats** and new **dresses** as well!

In the shoe shop, they asked if we would like to keep the **boxes**.

I decided the best **coats** would be nice cosy **fleeces**.

After the shopping I said, "Let's go to the café for warm **drinks**, shall we?" We took so long that we missed two **buses**!

Silent e

1.

a)   In winter I always wear a **hat**.
b)   I **woke** up at six o'clock today.
c)   A dog makes a good **pet**.
d)   Fir cones grow on a **pine** tree.
e)   The weather is **fine** today.
f)   I like bacon but I **hate** eggs.
g)   It is **time** to go to bed.
h)   I wrote a short **note**.
i)   The best fish to eat is **cod**.
j)   Children do not play **hide** and seek any more.
k)   I think mice are **cute**.
l)   Stir-fry is best cooked in a **wok**.

2.
I was **nine** when I first **rode** a **bike**. My **mate Luke gave** me his old Raleigh. He had won a new **bike** as a **prize** in a contest. I knew **Luke** would **like** the chance for us to **ride** together. So he **gave** me his old **bike**.
That old **bike became** my **pride** and joy. I put a new **tyre** on it. I polished the **chrome** to **make** it **shine**. I **made** it **nice**. Every **time** I'd been out for a **ride**, I **gave** it a clean. I spent all my **spare time** on that **bike**, and **gave** it lots of **care**. It was **mine**, you see.
At first when I **rode** my **bike**, it **made** my legs **ache**. As **time** went on they **became** strong, and soon I could **ride**

a **mile** or **more**. **Luke** and I **rode** up and down the **lane** till I knew I was **safe** to go further away from **home**.

Then we joined a club so we could get a much longer **ride**. One day Mr **Pike**, the man in **charge**, decided to **take** us to **Hope** **Dale** Picnic **Site**. The weather was warm and **fine**. We went all over the **countryside**, and **rode** all day. Then we had a swim in the **lake**, and lit a **fire** to **bake** some potatoes **before** we **came** **home**. I've never known anything **taste** so good.

When I was twelve I got a bigger, better **bike**, and again when I left school and got a **wage**. As I reached each new **stage** I would **change** my **bike**, and **move** on to another. It's been **like** that all my **life**.

I **dare** not tell you my **age**, but I still **like** to **ride**, come rain or **shine**. And I still have my old Raleigh **bike** **outside** in the shed. People **like** to **come** and see it. I **like** to see the **smile** on their **face** when they **stare** at my old **bike**.

3.
(Self-check)
Spelling method
(Self-check)
Suffixes

1.

a) rainy
b) gardener
c) careful, careless
d) kindness
e) breakable

f) friendship
g) attendance
h) hopeful, hopeless
i) surely
j) payment

2.

a) post, posts, posted, posting
b) care, cares, cared, caring, careful
c) fear, fears, feared, fearing, fearful, fearless
d) pave, paves, paved, paving, pavement
e) stop, stops, stopped, stopping
f) look, looks, looked, looking
g) regret, regrets, regretted
h) bet, bets, betted, betting, better
i) govern, governs, governed, government
j) improve, improves, improved, improvement
k) pot, pots, potting, potted
l) roast, roasts, roasted, roasting
m) step, steps, stepping, stepped
n) pass, passed, passing, passes
o) shop, shops, shopped, shopping
p) forget, forgetting, forgets, forgetful

Syllables,

1.
(Self-check)

2.
a) London: 2
b) college: 2
c) computer: 3
d) Leeds: 1
e) Denmark: 2
f) Manchester: 3
g) carpet: 2
h) table: 2
i) telephone: 3
j) me: 1
k) after: 2
l) like: 1
m) chocolate: 3
n) information: 4
o) essay: 2
p) classroom: 2
q) refectory: 4
r) exam: 2
s) paper: 2
t) university: 5

there, their, they're

1.
a) The college is over **there**.
b) **There** are plenty of spaces for parking.
c) Craig and Narina are eating **their** dinner.
d) **They're** taking an exam today.
e) **There** is no water in the kettle, and **there** are no tea-bags.
f) Sheep always know **their** own lambs.
g) **There** is a telephone call for you.

h) I left my book over **there**.

i) Students have **their** own lockers.

j) **They're** very lucky to have a locker each.

k) Last night **there** was a good programme on TV.

l) **They're** going to repeat it on Sunday.

2.

Most people these days have **their** own personal computer. This means that **they're** able to use the Internet and have **their** own e-mail address. They can do **their** shopping, organise **their** money, type **their** own letters and do many other wonderful things.

The world is changing, but **there** are some people who think that life was better before the days of the PC. They believe that **their** work was much simpler, and that **there** was a slower pace to life.

3.

There was no need for her to go out that day. **There** was plenty of food in the house, and **there** were no children to pick up from school. They were still with **their** grandparents. **There** were just the two of them. Tonight was **their** last chance.

they or there

1.

Last week my cat had kittens. **There** were five altogether. The mother cat carried them all into the airing cupboard because she knew **they** were safe and warm in **there**. **They** were all black and white, like their mother. When **they** are six weeks old I shall have to find homes for them. I will make sure **they** go to a very good home. I'm going to keep one, so **there** will only be four homes to find.

2.

There is an interesting family who live in that house over **there**. **They** have twins and triplets. The twins are boys. **They** are ten years old. **They** are identical. It's hard to tell who **they** are. **They** go everywhere together, and **they** do everything together. Then **there** are the triplets. **They** all have ginger hair, and **they** all look alike too. **They** are seven, and **they** are all girls. Their personalities seem different. Sometimes I can hear them when **they** are falling out with each other. But afterwards **they** make friends again. **They** are all nice children.

3.
I'm sure I left my keys over **there**, but **they** seem to be missing. **There** are four keys on the bunch, and **there** is a blue tag on the key-ring. **They** are the keys to my car and my house, so I need to find them. If you find them over **there**, could you let me know? Or **they** can be left with Reception. **There** is always someone **there**.

to, two or too
1.
a)   She is going **to** town.
b)   I have **two** children.
c)   It's **too** hot in here.
d)   I like cooking **too**.
e)   It's **two** o'clock.
f)   I am going **to** the dentist.
g)   My little boy is **two** years old.
h)   I have a daughter **too**.
i)   You work **too** hard.
j)   It's **too** late **to** go **to** the shop.
k)   I need **to** take your photo.
l)   There are **too** many people in the car.
m)   I need **to** go **to** bed.
n)   I have one or **two** books you might like.
o)   This tee-shirt is far **too** small.
p)   My coffee is **too** hot.

q)   I asked for **two** cups of tea.

2.
I am going **to** get up early tomorrow. I have **two** interesting things **to** do. First, I am going **to** a show. It starts at **two** o'clock. My sister is coming **too**. She has **two** dogs in the show.
This evening I am going with **two** friends **to** see a local band. We are going with **two** other people who I don't know. We are going in their car. Mine is **too** small. I hope the music isn't **too** loud!

Vowels
1.
a)   blackbird
b)   shopping
c)   marathon
d)   London
e)   college
f)   telephone
g)   encourage
h)   caravan
i)   sister
j)   brother
k)   swimming
l)   running
m)   carpet
n)   newspaper
o)   photograph
p)   employment
q)   Helen
r)   Jonathon
s)   touring
t)   emergency
u)   Colorado

2.

a)	cup	short
b)	paper:	long
c)	tea:	long
d)	sky:	long
e)	shape:	long
f)	John:	short
g)	sweet:	long
h)	waste:	long
i)	spot:	short
j)	post:	long
k)	pillow:	short
l)	bottle:	short
m)	computer:	long
n)	butter:	short
o)	metal:	short
p)	rabbit:	short
q)	tube:	long
r)	field:	long
s)	beetle:	long
t)	college:	short

we're, were or where

1.
a) I don't know **where** to look.
b) **We're** going on holiday tomorrow.
c) **Where** did you put the newspaper?
d) **Where** there is life, there is hope.
e) There **were** only two places left.
f) When you **were** a small child, you used to say funny things.
g) I'm not sure if **we're** supposed to be doing this.
h) I don't know **where** you live.
i) At one time there **were** fish in this river.
j) Next week **we're** having a party outside in the garden.
k) **We're** inviting all the neighbours.
l) Please put this **where** it will be safe.

m) We **were** hoping that you would be able to come to dinner.

n) I can't see **where** I'm going.

o) **We're** the best people for the job.

2.

"**Where** are we going?" I asked.

"**We're** going on a mystery tour," my sister replied.

"I thought we **were** going to London."

She laughed.

"Yes, I know you thought you **were** going to London!"

"Don't you know **where** the mystery tour is going?"

"No, **we're** having a surprise."

whose or who's

1.

a)   I don't know **whose** desk this is.

b)   **Who's** done that?

c)   **Who's** a clever girl, then?

d)   **Whose** car shall we go in?

e)   **Who's** that man over there?

f)   Do you know **whose** turn it is?

g)   We need to find out **who's** got a ticket.

h)   I need to know **who's** done this.

i)   **Who's** next, please?

j)   Please let me know **whose** team you are in.

k)   **Who's** the best person for the job?

l)   **Who's** been eating my porridge?

m)   **Who's** working on that computer?

n)   I'm not sure **whose** bag that is.

o)   I'll never know **who's** done this.

2.

"**Who's** written this?" I asked.

"I don't know **whose** writing that is," Ella replied, "but I know **who's** just bought a pen with purple ink!"

"**Who's** that?" I queried.

"The same person **who's** got a pad of pink paper."

"**Whose** pen is it?" I persisted, "and **whose** paper is it?"

"Look over there," Ella said, "and you'll soon know **whose** writing it is."

Words that look like 'though'

1.

a) I went **through** the door, and closed it behind me.

b) Have you **thought** about what you want to do?

c) I **thought** I might go on holiday.

d) The tutor's marking was very **thorough**.

e) I'd like to work in a big company, **though** there's always my dad's business which I **thought** I could try.

f) I had a very strange **thought** this morning.

g) I've worked **through** all the questions she set me.

h) He didn't win a prize, even **though** his entry was very good.

i) She's a **thorough** worker.

j) It was **through** my own fault that I missed the bus.

2.

It was a difficult and, I **thought**, a very interesting situation. I **thought** about it for a long time. I wanted to be very **thorough**. Then I realised that I needed to talk it **through** with someone. I **thought** about who could help me, **though** deep down I knew I would have to sort it out myself.

'y' plurals

1.

a) A ferry, two **ferries**

b) The lorry, a fleet of **lorries**

c) One boy, three **boys**

d) A red jelly, a choice of **jellies**

e) One day, seven **days**

f) A calamity, a series of **calamities**
g) A political party, all the political **parties**
h) One guy, two **guys**
i) A motorway, Britain's **motorways**
j) A good hobby, some good **hobbies**

2.
4 Cornish **pasties**
Pkt baps for bacon **butties**
4 Danish **pastries**
4 gingerbread **teddies**
2 vegetable **curries**
2 Cadbury's Milk **Trays**
6 children's **lollies**
Pkt toffee **candies**
Some little **toys** for the kids.
2 Matthews' frozen **turkeys**
Pkt frozen French **fries**
2 orange **jellies**
Bottle cocktail **cherries**
Box paper **hankies**
Pack disposable **nappies**
2 different **honeys**
Punnet **strawberries**
4 Size C **batteries**
2 new **keys** cut at kiosk

P.S. Park next to where the **trolleys** are – that's where the bottle bank is so you can throw away the **empties**. And could you find a DVD with children's **stories** on it please? Thanks.

your or you're

1.
a) Is that **your** car?
b) Please turn **your** computer off.

c)   I think **you're** a wonderful person.
d)   What is **your** name?
e)   **You're** quite right about that.
f)   I think I know **your** sister.
g)   **You're** doing really well with that.
h)   Is this **your** coat?
i)   **You're** on the wrong train!
j)   Do you know where **you're** going?
k)   Shall we go to **your** house?
l)   It was **your** idea.

2.
Now that **you're** getting older, I would like to tell you about **your** grandfather. **You're** very like him. **Your** hair is exactly the same colour as his was, and **your** eyes too. **You're** also very similar in **your** looks. I see **you're** interested in animals, just as he was. I sometimes wonder if **you're** going to be a vet, too, and make **your** living from it like **your** grandfather did. I know you will do **your** best, whatever **your** choice. It's the way **you're** made.